THE
PROMETHEUS BOUND
OF AESCHYLUS

THE
PROMETHEUS
BOUND
OF AESCHYLUS

a translation by

REX WARNER

THE BODLEY HEAD · LONDON

First published 1947

Printed in Great Britain by
UNWIN BROTHERS LIMITED, LONDON AND WOKING
for THE BODLEY HEAD LIMITED
8 Bury Place London WC1

THE CHARACTERS

PROMETHEUS, *the Titan*

IO

OKEANOS, *god of the Ocean*

HERMES, *messenger of Zeus*

HEPHAISTOS, *god of Fire*

POWER

VIOLENCE

and

CHORUS OF THE DAUGHTERS OF OKEANOS

The Story

THE story of the PROMETHEUS BOUND of Aeschylus is, on the face of it, a simple one. Prometheus, the Titan, is one of those rather shadowy divine powers who were in existence before Zeus conquered his father Kronos and established himself as dictator of the gods. Unlike the rest of the older gods, Prometheus went over to the side of Zeus and it was partly owing to his advice that Zeus was successful in gaining absolute power. Prometheus (the name means 'fore-thought') differed from his brothers in having grasped the fact that intelligence, not brute force, was to be the governing power of the universe. Also he was the champion of mankind. Zeus had wished to destroy men utterly and make another race instead. Prometheus saved them from this fate and went further still. He initiated men into all the arts and sciences which make civilisation possible and, to secure his object of raising mankind from the beasts, he stole from heaven the gods' prerogative of fire, and gave this final gift to men.

For this he was seized by Zeus and bound in fetters on a rocky mountain. It is at this point that the play starts. Hephaistos, the god of fire, unwillingly executes the order of his master, Zeus. Prometheus complains of the ingratitude and the injustice shown by 'the new dictator of the gods.' He is comforted in his misfortunes by the daughters of Ocean, representatives, like himself, of the old order, before Zeus established his power.

There is little obvious 'action' in the play. Ocean himself comes and attempts to persuade Prometheus that it is a wise thing to submit to the powers that be, and his advice is proudly rejected. Prometheus is strong in the possession of a secret. Zeus, he knows, will, unless warned of it, make a marriage

7

from which will come a son mightier than the father, and Prometheus is determined not to divulge the secret. Then, arriving as it were by accident, there appears another victim of Zeus's injustice, Io, a girl who has been selected as Zeus's paramour, driven out of her home, given the shape of a heifer, and is now pursued from country to country by a gad-fly. All this is the direct result of the jealousy of Hera, Zeus's wife, yet, indirectly, Io's sufferings are plainly caused by Zeus himself. Io continues on her wanderings after Prometheus has given her an account of both her future and his own.

Then Hermes, the messenger of Zeus, arrives and demands to know the secret of which Prometheus has been boasting. If Prometheus remains oburate, sufferings far worse than his present ones will be let loose upon him. He will be plunged beneath the earth in an earthquake and at length brought back to the light, when, day after day, an eagle will come and gnaw his continually restored liver. Prometheus is wholly unmoved by threats. He will resist to the end, and the play closes in thunder and lightning and convulsions of the earth.

Problems of the Story

ON the face of it the play appears as a glorification of the revolutionary who, strong in his own mind and convinced of the justice of his cause, will never bow to oppression. This version of its meaning has always appealed to romantic revolutionaries, and is best shown in Shelley's PROMETHEUS UNBOUND. It is not, however, the whole story according to Aeschylus. The PROMETHEUS BOUND is only one play in a trilogy, and neither of the

8

other two plays survives. We do know, however, that in Aeschylus's PROMETHEUS UNBOUND there has been a reconciliation between the apparently irreconcilable forces represented by Prometheus and Zeus. Precisely how this reconciliation took place we do not know, but, from our knowledge of Aeschylus's way of thought, it seems fair to assume that the reconciliation was the result of some compromise or development by which Zeus, growing wiser, became less tyrannical and Prometheus came to recognise that an attitude of mere defiance, however splendid, is ineffective.

To Aeschylus, therefore, Prometheus is not, as he was to Shelley, the perfect hero. He is certainly a grand and sympathetic figure,—as grand as and more sympathetic than Milton's Satan, that other cosmic revolutionary. Right—ordinary human right—seems to be on his side. By all human standards Zeus is behaving monstrously. Yet it is a fact that nature, and what the Greeks called 'necessity' do not proceed in accordance with human standards of justice and morality and, so Aeschylus seems to suggest, a failure to recognise this is a dangerous and unjustifiable form of pride. Not that this suggestion is any solution to the main problem. A solution to the problem of the evident inhumanity of the processes of the universe must lie somewhere beyond reason in a faith that somehow and somewhere injustice will be found to have been justified in the end. So Io's misfortunes will not last for ever. Finally she will give birth immaculately to the child of Zeus, and Prometheus himself will be restored to his old honours.

But there is more than this in Aeschylus's thought. Though he makes it clear that rebellions against God can never be finally justified, he, no less than Shelley, shows the grandeur of such a rebellion as that of Prometheus. Though Prometheus is proud, he is certainly heroic. Moreover the effect of his splendid sin is, after years of suffering, to produce a change in the nature of God himself. The very idea of such a change in 'eternal change-

9

lessness' seems impossible to us, but it must be remembered that in the confused Greek mythology there were a succession of supreme beings, and the possibilities of even omnipotence changing its form or omniscience yielding to persuasion might be considered and debated.

Enough, however, has been said to show that this play, in spite of its great romantic appeal, is not merely the glorification of a romantic idea. It is an investigation into the problem of the injustice of life and, since the rest of the trilogy is lost, it is a partial investigation. It is a play where the 'action' is supplied by symbols of philosophical ideas, where the interest is allegorical and the meaning somewhere rather beyond the words, prophetic, as is the style and thought of this great dramatist.

The PROMETHEUS BOUND
of AESCHYLUS

★

[*A savage scene in mountains.*
Enter Hephaistos, with Power and
Violence, who are leading Prometheus.]

POWER

Now we have come to the plain at the end of the earth,
the Scythian tract, and an untrodden wilderness.
And you, Hephaistos, must turn your mind to the orders
the father gave you,—to discipline and pin down
this outlaw here upon the lofty ragged rocks
in unbreakable bonds of adamantine chains.
It was your flower, the gleam of civilising fire,
he stole and handed it over to mortals. Therefore
he must pay the price of such a sin to the gods,
that he may be taught to bend to the dictatorship
of Zeus, and give up his ideas of helping men.

HEPHAISTOS

Power and Violence, for you the command of Zeus
has reached fulfilment. There is nothing left to do.
But I have not the heart to bind a brother god
violently to this stormy cleft in the mountains.
Yet every way I am forced to find the heart for it,
since it is hard to leave undone the father's word.

[*He turns to Prometheus.*]

O you deep-scheming son of rightminded Themis,
against your will and mine with ineluctable brass
I am nailing you down to this rock away from men,
Where you will never hear the voice or see the sight
of any mortal, and, scorched by the sun's bright fire,
the flower of your flesh will shrivel, and you will be glad
when rich-clothed night shall hide away the day, and when
once more the sun scatters the frost at dawn. Always
the load of what you suffer at the moment will
oppress you, since your saviour has not yet been born.
This is your reward for your idea of helping men.
Yourself a god, you did not shrink from wrath of gods,
and gave to man promotion beyond what is right.
And therefore you will now be sentry of this joyless rock,
standing upright, not sleeping, not bending the knee.
There will be many sighs and many useless groans
that you will utter. Zeus's mind is hard to turn
by prayer, and all whose power is new are hard hearted.

POWER

Enough of this. Why the delay? Why the empty pity?
Why do you not hate the god most hated by the gods,
the one who betrayed to men your own prerogative?

HEPHAISTOS

There's a strange force in kinship and fellow-feeling.

POWER

I agree. But to leave unheard the father's command,
how is that possible? Do you not fear that more?

HEPHAISTOS

Oh, you are pitiless always and empty of feeling.

12

POWER

Yes, since there is no cure in singing dirges for him.
Waste not your own trouble on what will do no good.

HEPHAISTOS

O my master skill of the hand, how much I hate you!

POWER

And why hate that? Your skill, if I may put it plainly,
has nothing whatever to do with your present trouble.

HEPHAISTOS

Still I wish it had fallen to another, not me.

POWER

All things are burdensome, except power over gods,
since there is no one except Zeus who has freedom.

HEPHAISTOS

I know it by these chains, and have no more to say.

POWER

Then be quick to throw the bonds around this man here,
lest the father look upon you and find you idling.

HEPHAISTOS

Here, ready to our hands are the chains for checking him.

POWER

Throw them about his arms! In your powerful strength
strike, strike with the hammer! Nail him to the rocks!

HEPHAISTOS

This work is nearly done, and is not done in vain.

POWER

Strike harder! Press the bonds tight, and leave nothing loose.
He is one to find ways out even from hopelessness.

HEPHAISTOS

This arm at least is fixed and hard to be released.

POWER

And now pin down the other fast, that he may know
his brilliant mind moves slower than the mind of Zeus.

HEPHAISTOS

No one but he can have the right to reproach me.

POWER

Now the unfeeling tooth of a spike of adamant!
Use all your strength and nail it right through his breast!

HEPHAISTOS

Alas, Prometheus! I am sorry for your pain.

POWER

Will you shrink back and be sorry for Zeus's enemies?
Take care. You may have to moan for yourself one day.

HEPHAISTOS

You see a sight most hard for eyes to look upon.

POWER

I see one here who is getting what he deserves.
Come, fasten about his body the restraining bonds.

HEPHAISTOS

I am forced to do this. Do not urge me on too far.

POWER

Be sure I'll urge you and shout encouragement besides.
Go down, put rings of violence about his legs!

HEPHAISTOS

See now, the task is done, and did not take too long.

POWER

Now use your strength and strike the bolts in the fetters.
Hard, as you know, is the overseer of this work.

HEPHAISTOS

All of a piece the words of your tongue and your shape.

POWER

Be soft yourself, but as for my unyieldingness
and my toughness of temper, do not blame them on me.

HEPHAISTOS

Let us go. Now he has the chains about his limbs.

POWER [speaking to Prometheus]

Now, where you are, behave outrageously and steal
and give to things of a day prerogatives of gods!
Can mortals help you out from any of these pains?
The gods who called you 'Forethought' gave you a false name.
You need forethought yourself if you would find a way
to break out into freedom from this work of art.

[Hephaistos, Power and Violence go, leaving Prometheus alone.]

PROMETHEUS

O heavenly air, and breezes swift upon the wing,
fountains of rivers and innumerable laughter

of the waves of the sea, and earth, mother of all,
and you, all-seeing circle of the sun, I call,
see what I suffer, a god at the hand of gods.
O see in what bitter shame,
worn out through the countless years,
my race is set.
This is the bondage of shame for me
found out by the new lord of the blessed gods.
Alas, alas, I cry for the woe that is here,
for the woe that is coming, and where will they ever,
my torments, be destined to come to an end?
Yet what is this I say? I know what is coming,
all of it exactly, and not a single evil
can reach me unforeseen, and I must bear the fate
allotted to me as best I may, because I know
one cannot fight with the power of necessity.
Yet neither silence nor full speech is possible
for me in these misfortunes. For giving to men
God's gift I am tied down wretched in compulsion.
For I am he who sought the stolen fount of fire,
stored in a stalk, which proved to be the teacher of
all kind of craft to mortals and their great resource.
This was the sin for which I pay the punishment
nailed hard and fast in chains beneath the open sky.

[*a sound of wings is heard. It is the chorus of the daughters of
Okeanos, who have come to comfort him.*]

Ah, what is the sound and what is the fragrance
that floats to me viewless?
Is it of gods or of mortals or both?
Has one come to this rock at the end of the world
to survey my disaster, or why has he come?
You see me a captive, a god ill-fated,

16

Zeus's enemy, one grown hateful
to everyone of the gods who enters
Zeus's palace, because of my
excessive kindness to men.
O what can it be that I hear close by me?
The rustle of bird-wings? With light beat of feathers
all the air trembles, and all that comes near me
is matter for fear.

CHORUS

Fear no danger. It is a troop of friends
which in quick rivalry
of wing has reached this rock, and hardly won
by prayer the father's mind to let us come.
Swift-speeding breezes have borne me.
Through cavern depths there pierced the sound of a blow
of iron and summoned forth my shame grave-eyed.
With feet unsandalled in my wingéd car I came.

PROMETHEUS

Alas!
You children of Tethys, mother of many,
daughters of old father Okeanos,
he who with sleepless stream engirdles
all of the world,
look at me, see in what cruel bondage,
nailed to the topmost crags of this mountain,
I shall watch here unenvied.

CHORUS

I see, Prometheus, and a mist of fear
has leapt upon my eyes,
a mist that's full of tears, when I look
upon your body wasting on the rocks

P.B.   17   B

in infamous bondage of adamant.
New rulers now hold power in Olympus,
and in new-fangled law Zeus blindly lords it.
Titanic powers of old can now be seen no more.

PROMETHEUS

I wish he had hurled me under the earth,
lower than Hades, keeper of corpses,
into the limitless gulf of Tartaros,
In cruel bondage of chains unbreakable,
so neither god nor any creature
had joyed in my sorrow.
Now in my misery made air's plaything,
I suffer what pleases my foes.

CHORUS

No god is so hard hearted
as to be pleased with this.
All are indignant at your wrongs,
all except Zeus, and he,
ever angry with a mind set,
never bending, crushes down the sons
of Ouranos, nor will he cease before he sates his heart,
or by some force another steals his empire hard to win.

PROMETHEUS

Still I can swear to you that the president
of the immortals will find out his need for me,
for all the maltreatment of these strong chains.
He will need me to tell the new plan by whose working
he will be stripped of his sceptre and honour.
And then by no honey-tongued charms of persuasion
will he win my mind over.
Nor shall I ever shrink from his terrible

18

threats and reveal it,
till he has loosed me from these cruel chains,
and is willing to pay
recompense for my shame.

CHORUS

O you are bold, unyielding
in all your bitter pain;
Your speech's freedom goes too far.
A piercing fear is stirring
up my heart, and for your fortune
terror fills me, and I know not where
fate will have you end your voyage and see the end of pain.
Mood immovable and heart of stone has Kronos' son.

PROMETHEUS

I know of his harshness, I know that Zeus measures
what is just by his interest. And yet
soft-minded he will be
in time, broken down as I say.
He will settle his obstinate anger.
As eager as I in time he will come
claiming peace and alliance.

CHORUS

Uncover everything and tell us all the story.
What was the accusation on which Zeus took you,
and now so bitterly and shamefully wrongs you?
Tell us, if nothing prevents you from the telling.

PROMETHEUS

It causes pain to me even to tell the story,
and there is pain in silence. Each way is misery.
Now, first, when the gods entered upon their anger,

19

when they split into parties, and strife rose among them,
some wishing to cast Kronos out of his empire,
so that this Zeus of ours might reign, and the others
as eager to prevent Zeus ever ruling gods,—
at this time, though I planned to give the best counsel
to my Titan brothers, children of Heaven and Earth,
my effort was unavailing. In their proud minds
they saw no place for the trickery of intelligence:
by right of might they assumed they would rule unchallenged.
But to me my mother Themis, and not once only,
and Gaia, one person beneath the varied names,
had foretold what was the future dispensation—
that the way of fate was not by strength or force of might:
victory and power proceeded from intelligence.
But when I had set out this before them in words,
they thought it all not worth a moment's attention.
So, with all this before me then, what seemed the best
was to take my mother with me and show that good will
which Zeus showed too, and take my stand together with him.
By my device it was the deep dark hiding place
of Hell now covers up, with all who fought with him,
Old Kronos. And now the dictator of the gods,
after receiving all this benefit from me,
has paid me back with bitter wrong that you behold.
This is a sickness, it seems, that goes along with
dictatorship—inability to trust one's friends.
Now for your question, which was—on what accusation
he now maltreats me. This I shall make plain to you.
When first he took his seat upon his father's throne,
he divided out at once the various privileges
to the gods in turn and brought his empire into shape.
As for long suffering men, he took no care at all;
indeed his plan was to make the whole of their race
extinct and then to form another race instead.

20

Except for me no one opposed his purpose here.
I dared to stand against him and I saved mankind
from being broken to pieces and sent down to Hell.
For this, I tell you, I am bowed in sufferings
painful to feel and pitiful to look upon.
When I felt pity first for mortals I thought not
that I would be the sufferer, yet, as you see,
I am forced to harmony, a sight of shame for Zeus.

CHORUS

Of iron heart, Prometheus, fashioned out of rock
must be the man who shares not your indignation
at your hard toil. I would not have chosen to see
a sight like this, and, seeing it, my heart is sore.

PROMETHEUS

For friends to see, yes, I am one to be pitied.

CHORUS

But did you not perhaps go further than all this?

PROMETHEUS

Yes. I stopped mortals from seeing their fate in advance.

CHORUS

What cure did you find to charm away that sickness?

PROMETHEUS

I settled unseeing hopes to dwell among them.

CHORUS

Here was great kindness in the gift you gave to men.

PROMETHEUS

And after that I gave to them the gift of fire.

CHORUS

Do creatures of a day now own the flame-faced fire?

PROMETHEUS

They do, and they will learn from it all kinds of arts.

CHORUS

Is this, then, all the accusation for which Zeus—

PROMETHEUS

Maltreats me, and in no way grants a pause from suffering.

CHORUS

Is there laid down no ending-place for your ordeal?

PROMETHEUS

No end at all, except when it seems good to Zeus.

CHORUS

How can that ever be? What hope is there? Do you not see
you were wrong? In what way wrong it hurts me to say,
and gives you no pleasure either. Let us leave
that subject. Try to find release from your ordeal.

PROMETHEUS

It is a light thing for those who take their stand outside
the place where evil is to give advice to one
who feels the evil. I knew of all this before.
I did the wrong, and meant it, and I admit it.
In helping mortals I found trouble for myself,
though I never thought that in such punishment as this,

22

upon these airy cliffs, that I should waste away,
my portion being the unneighboured desolate rock.
So do not weep for the pain I feel at present.
Come down to earth, listen as I tell of the moving
forward of fate, and hear the story to the end.
Come, listen to me, as I ask. Show fellow-feeling
for one who is now unhappy. Suffering roves
from one to another, and settles on all alike.

CHORUS

We are willing, Prometheus,
to do as you tell us,
and now on a light foot, leaving my rushing
chariot and holy
bird-path of air, I
come to this rough rock, and long
to hear all the tale of your sorrow.

[Enter Okeanos on a winged monster.]

OKEANOS

At the end of the long road,
Prometheus, I come to you,
and steer by my will, without any bridle,
this wing-swift flyer.
Be sure that I grieve with you in your misfortunes.
Kinship, I know, must
force me to do so;
but, apart from all blood-ties, I know of no one
for whom I would wish to do more than for you.
You will realise the truth of my words, since I cannot
speak fair and not mean fair.
Now tell me how you wish me to help you.
You will never be able to say that you have
a friend truer than I am.

23

PROMETHEUS

Now what is this I see? It is you who have come
to look upon my pain? How did you find the heart
to leave the stream you name, the self-made vaulted caves
of rock, and come to the earth, the mother of iron?
Was it to be spectator of these my sufferings,
and to join me in indignation that you came?
Here is the sight to see—it is I, the friend of Zeus,
the one who helped him establish his dictatorship,
in suffering he sent upon me now bowed down.

OKEANOS

I see it, Prometheus, and, though I know your subtle mind,
I wish to give to you the best advice I can.
Recognise your own weakness, learn to adapt your ways
to new ways. In heaven we have a new dictator.
For, if you hurl abroad these bitter razor-edged words,
Zeus, though his throne is far above you, may hear you,
and then all this crowd of trouble which you have now
will come to seem to you nothing more than child's play.
No, my poor friend, put aside the anger you feel,
and try to find a way of release from your pain.
You may think the words I speak to you old-fashioned,
and yet, Prometheus, such sufferings as these ones
are the usual wages of tongues that speak too proudly.
You are not yet humble, you do not yet give way
to your affliction. Instead you seek more still of it.
So, if you listen to the advice I give to you,
you will not kick against the pricks, in the knowledge
that a stern monarch rules with power uncontrolled.
Now I shall go my way and shall, if I am able,
attempt to win for you release from your pain.
You must lie low and check the pride of your language.
I am sure that you, so wise, know this for a fact—

the reward of empty language is always punishment.

PROMETHEUS

I envy you your luck in being free from blame,
though you dared all and took your share in all with me.
Now leave things as they are, do not concern yourself.
You will never persuade him. He is not to be won over.
Look close to yourself, lest you suffer by your errand.

OKEANOS

You are far better at giving advice to others
than to yourself, and here I judge by facts not words.
Yet now I have started, do not pull me back again,
since I am sure and confident that Zeus will give
this gift to me, to free you from your sufferings.

PROMETHEUS

For this I am grateful to you, and always will be.
You show no lack of any willingness to help.
Yet do not trouble. Wasteful and profitless will be
the trouble you take for me, if you must take it.
Lie low, I say, and keep yourself out of harm's way.
I am not one who, just because of my ill-luck,
would wish unhappy as many others as might be.
Far from it. The sorrows too of my brother Atlas
afflict me, Atlas who in regions of the West
stands still and bears upon his shoulders the pillar
of heaven and earth, no easy burden on the arms.
Yes, and I pitied when I saw him the earth-born
dweller in the Cilician caves, the terrible
monster, the hundred-headed one, laid low by force,
furious Typhon, who took his stand against the whole

25

of heaven, and hissed out horror from his grisly jaws,
and from his eyes he flashed grim-visaged gleam of fire,
bent to destroy by force the tyranny of Zeus.
But the unsleeping bolt of Zeus came down on him,
the precipitous thunder-stone, breathing out fire,
and knocked the proud words out of him and the boasting.
Struck through to the very heart he became mere dust
and ashes, and his strength was blasted out of him.
Now useless to him, stretched out at length, his body
lies by the narrow Mediterranean waters
weighed down beneath the weight of the roots of Etna.
And, sitting on the peaks, Hephaistos forges masses
of molten metal, and from these one day will burst
rivers of fire, devouring with their savage jaws
the smooth Sicilian meadows in that land of fruit.
So Typhon, in hot heavings of insatiable
fire-breathing spray will force his anger boiling up,
though burnt to ashes by the thunderbolt of Zeus.
You are not ignorant. You have no need of me
to be your teacher. Save yourself, as you know how to.
And I shall fulfil to the end my present fortune,
until the mind of Zeus shall rest from its anger.

OKEANOS

This point, Prometheus, you must recognise,—that words
can act like medicine for a spirit in distress.

PROMETHEUS

Yes, if one soothes the heart when the heart is ripe for it,
not if one represses by force a bursting anger.

OKEANOS

Tell me, what is the punishment you see involved
in being willing to help, and in showing daring?

26

PROMETHEUS

Excessive trouble and empty-headed simplicity.

OKEANOS

Let me then suffer from this sickness, since I know
the safest thing is to be wise and not thought wise.

PROMETHEUS

That is an error for which I shall have the blame.

OKEANOS

Your words are plainly sending me back home again.

PROMETHEUS

Yes, in case your pity for me should bring you hatred.

OKEANOS

From him who newly sits upon the almighty throne?

PROMETHEUS

Yes, watch him, in case one day his heart grows angry.

OKEANOS

Your own fortune, Prometheus, is my instructor.

PROMETHEUS

Now go, set off, keep to the purpose you have now.

OKEANOS

You urge me on now that I am about to go.
My four-foot flyer with his wings brushes the smooth
paths of the air, and he will, I know, be happy
to bend his knee again in the familiar stable.

[*Okeanos goes away on his winged monster.*]

27

Weeping for you, your deadly fate, Prometheus,
Welling with tears, down from my delicate eyes
shedding the stream, I wet
my cheek with dewy fountains.
Here Zeus unhappily
rules by the laws he made himself,
to the gods of old revealing
arrogant tyranny.

Now the whole earth has raised a cry of mourning.
All men lament the dying out of the splendid
time-honoured noble fame
of yours and of your brothers.
All mortals dwelling in
houses and homes of holy Asia
in your hard grievous suffering
weep and lament with you,

and the maidens who are fearless in the fight,
they who dwell in Kolchis' land,
and the hordes who are in Scythia, and there
at the furthest point of earth
live around Maeotis' lake;

and the battle-honoured flower of Aria,
men who hold by Caucasus
their precipitous and rocky citadel,
savage armies roaring out
in the biting of the blade.

I saw before one other Titan god,
and one alone so broken down in pain.
It was tremendous Atlas, ever strong,
who, groaning, bears upon his back
earth and the heavenly pole.

The ocean wave breaks in a roar of woe,
the deep sea groans, and the black hole of hell
mutters beneath the earth, and all the fountains
of lucid-flowing rivers mourn
in pity for your pain.

PROMETHEUS

Think not that I am silent because of arrogance
or stubbornness. No, it is thought consumes my mind
when I look upon myself insulted as I am.
Yet who was it but I who, from the first to the last,
handed out to these new gods of ours their honours?
Enough of that. I should be telling that story
to you who know it. Listen though to the sufferings
in mortals—how I found them all helpless at first,
and made them able to reflect and use their wits.
I shall tell the story, not from any grudge to men,
but simply to declare the kindness of my gifts.
They, then, at first had eyes, but all their sight was vain;
they had ears, but did not hear. Instead they were like
the shapes we see in dreams, and all through their long life
they mingled all things aimlessly, and never knew of
houses, brick-built and warm, or the art of wood-work.
They lived in burrows, like the light and nimble ants
down in the deep sunless recesses of their caves.
Nor had they any certain sign by which to know
the times of winter, spring with its flowers, or fruitful
summer. Instead they acted in every matter
without intelligence, till I revealed to them
the risings of the stars and settings hard to judge.
And then I found for them the art of using numbers,
that master science, and arrangement of letters,
and a discursive memory, a skill to be
mother of muses. I was first to bring the beasts

to serve under the yoke and saddle, that they might
take on themselves the greatest burdens of mortals.
And it was I who brought, and made them love the rein,
horses to chariots, the pride of lordly wealth.
And no one else but I discovered for sailors
the sea-wandering vessels with their canvas wings.
These were the arts I, foolish I, devised for men,
and for myself I have no device of science
by which to escape from the suffering I feel now.

CHORUS

You have suffered shamefully, and now you are astray,
driven out of your wits, and, like some bad physician,
fallen ill, you lose your courage and know not yourself
and how to find the drugs by which you can be cured.

PROMETHEUS

When you have heard my tale out, you will wonder more
at all the arts I discovered and the sciences.
This was the greatest. In the past, when men fell ill,
there was nothing to help them, no food they might take,
no ointment for the skin, or medicine to drink.
Through lack of drugs they withered away, until I
showed them the ingredients of soothing medicines
by means of which they keep all illnesses at bay.
Then I laid down the lines of many ways of prophecy.
I first discerned from dreams the elements destined
to be true in waking life, and of sounds hard to judge,
I taught the interpreting, and I clearly defined
omens met in the way, the flight of crook-clawed birds,
which ones were of the lucky sort, and the others
unlucky, and the way of living each kind had,
what enmities there were between the different kinds,
what bonds of friendship and what associations.

30

I taught men too about the smoothness of entrails
and of what colour they should be to please the gods,
the auspicious shape of the gall-bladder and liver.
And then, by burning fat-enveloped limbs and loins
of sacrifices, I set mortals on the path
of a science hard to judge, and to the signs in flames
I made their eyes bright that before were dim and dark.
So much for these things. Then what was beneath the earth
stored up and hidden for the benefit of men,
bronze, iron, silver, gold,—who is there who could claim
to have found all these out before me? No one could,
no one, unless he wished to make an empty boast.
In this short word learn all the story together:
Prometheus gave all arts and sciences to men.

CHORUS

In doing good to mortals now unseasonably
do not forget yourself and your misfortunes. I
am full of hope that a day will come when you,
freed from these chains, will hold a power no less than Zeus.

PROMETHEUS

No, not yet is fulfilling Fate fixed to accomplish
things in this way. Instead bowed down by innumerable
sufferings and pains, thus only shall I win freedom.
Science is weaker a long way than necessity.

CHORUS

Whose hand is it that holds the tiller of necessity?

PROMETHEUS

The threefold Fates, and the remembering Erinyes.

31

CHORUS

Is Zeus, then, weaker than the Fates and Erinyes?

PROMETHEUS

He will not run away from what Fate has in store.

CHORUS

But what is Zeus's fate except to rule always?

PROMETHEUS

You must not learn this yet, so do not seek to know.

CHORUS

This is some holy secret which you fold away.

PROMETHEUS

Think of some other thing to tell. The time is not
ripe for revealing this. Instead it must be hidden
as far as possible, for, if I keep this secret,
I shall escape my shameful bondage and my pain.

CHORUS

O never may Zeus, who holds the sway over all,
set his might counter to my desire.
Never may I be slow to approach the gods
by the ever-flowing path of father Okeanos
with the holy sacrifices of stricken bulls.
Never may I in word
fall into sin. O let
this resolution stay
fixed in my heart and never melt away.

Sweet it is to go through the length of life
in confident hope, cheering the heart with bright

shining of joy. But, oh, when I look on you
wasting away in innumerable labours,
I tremble at the sight I see, Prometheus.
You have no fear of Zeus,
but, following the way
of a private judgment, you
give honour in excess to mortal men.

O see what a gift that recoiled on the giver was that.
What help is there anywhere, friend?
What support from these things of a day? O did you not notice
an impotent helplessness, weak as a dream,
in which the blind tribe of mankind
is fettered and bound?
Never shall plans made by mortals
go beyond the fixed pattern of Zeus.

This was the lesson, Prometheus, I learned when I saw
this deadly disaster of yours.
O how different the song that has leapt to my lips from the
    song
I sang in delight at your wedding and bed
of your bride and ablutions, when you
won the heart of my sister
by your bride-gifts and brought her to be
the wife who would sleep at your side.

[Enter Io.]

IO

Where am I? Who lives here? Who shall I say
is this that I see in fetters of rock
exposed to the storm?
For what sin are you paying atonement?
Tell me where I have wandered,
poor wretch as I am.

Ah, ah,
again some biting fly stings my poor body.
It is the ghost of earth-born Argos. Keep,
keep him away, O Earth. I am afraid,
seeing the herdsman with his myriad eyes.
He stalks here with his cunning look, and even in death
Earth will not cover him; no, me, poor me
he rises from the dead to hunt, and drives me
wandering and hungry by the sand of the sea.

And meanwhile sounds the wax-made shrill
pipe a lullaby measure. O alas!
Where are they taking me, my far-wandering ways?
Whatever was it, O son of Kronos, I did?
When did you find me at fault that you tied me down,
Oh, to this pain,
and wear me away, poor thing, all crazy now
in fear of the stinging fly?
Burn me with fire, hide me in earth, and give me
for food to sea-monsters.
O hear my prayer, master!
My far-ranging courses
are discipline enough, nor can I tell
how to escape my pain.
Do you hear the voice of the girl with horns like a cow?

PROMETHEUS

I hear the maid who is driven by the stinging fly,
Inachos' daughter, she who melts the heart of Zeus
in love, and now, hated by Hera, violently
is disciplined in courses that have no ending.

IO

How can you give my father's name?
Tell me, poor me, who can you be, O sad

sight that you are, to name so truly a poor
maid, and to tell of the sickness that wastes me away,
goading me on with its, ah! with its maddening stings.
Swiftly I came
sped to leap with the bitter hungry ache
and tamed by Hera's angry
plotting. O which of the wretched are there, which
who suffer as I do?
But tell me now plainly
What more must I suffer,
or what help is there and relief from sickness.
Reveal it, if you know.
Speak, answer the girl who has wandered unhappily here.

PROMETHEUS

All that you wish to know I will tell you clearly,
not weaving riddles, but in a straight forward speech,
which is the right way to talk in front of one's friends.
You see the giver of fire to men—Prometheus.

IO

O poor Prometheus, you who showed yourself to be
a blessing shared by all men, why do you suffer so?

PROMETHEUS

Just now I ceased wailing over my sufferings.

IO

Will you not give me, then, this gift I ask of you?

PROMETHEUS

Say what it is you want. You will learn all from me.

35

IO

Tell who it was who nailed you in this mountain cleft.

PROMETHEUS

Zeus made the plan. Hephaistos carried out the work.

IO

What was the sin for which you are being punished?

PROMETHEUS

What I have said already is enough to say.

IO

Yet tell me more. Tell what the limit will be to
my wandering, and what the time set to my pain.

PROMETHEUS

It is better for you not to know this than to know it.

IO

Do not hide from me what I am going to suffer.

PROMETHEUS

Not that I grudge the giving of this gift to you.

IO

Why, then, do you hold back from telling me it all?

PROMETHEUS

Not from ill-feeling: but I shrink from maddening you.

IO

Take no more thought for me than I myself desire.

Since you will have it so, then I must speak. Now listen.

CHORUS

Yet wait, and give to me my share of pleasure too.
First let us ask her of the sickness she suffers,
and let her tell herself of her destructive fate.
Then she may learn the rest of her trials from you.

PROMETHEUS

It is for you, Io, to do this kindness to them.
Remember, too, they are sisters of your father.
And time is well spent in grief and lamentation
over one's fortune in the kind of company
where one will win a tear from those who listen to you.

IO

I do not see how I can fail to do your will.
You will hear in plain words all that you wish to know,
though even in speaking of it I feel the pain
of the storm god launched upon me, and the change of shape,
how it came suddenly on me, poor thing that I am.
There were always visions haunting my virgin bed
night after night, and speaking kindly in my ears
with smooth words saying: 'O most fortunate maiden,
why keep so long your maidenhood, when you might make
the greatest match? Zeus is on fire with a shaft
of longing for you, and wants to join in love with you.
It is not for you, my child, to spurn aside the bed
of Zeus. No, you must go out in the deep meadow
of Lerna, to your father's herds and cattle stalls,
so that the eye of Zeus may rest from its desire.'
And I, poor I, by dreams like these through every hour
of sleep was hard beset till the time I had courage

to tell my father of the fears that came by night.
Then he despatched to Pytho and to Dodona
numerous messengers to find out what was right
for him to do or say to suit the will of heaven.
And they came back with messages of shifting speech,
obscurely spoken oracles and hard to judge.
Finally Inachos received a clear reply
giving him a plain injunction and commanding him
to thrust me out of my home and out of my land,
and set me loose to wander to the ends of earth.
And, if he would not do it, then from Zeus would come
the fire-faced thunderbolt to wipe out all his race.
By this reply of Loxias his mind was swayed:
he drove me into exile, locked me out of home.
It was against his will and mine, but Zeus's bridle
put violent stress on him to do as he did.
And immediately both my shape and my mind were changed.
As you see, I grew horns. Stung by the sharp-mouthed fly
I darted leaping madly onward till I came
to the pleasant waters of the stream of Kerchneia,
and to Lerna's fountain. And the earth-born cattle man,
untempered in his anger, Argos, followed after,
looking along my tracks with all his many eyes.
There came on him a sudden unexpected fate
and robbed him of his life. But I, stung by the fly,
beneath the whip of heaven am forced from land to land.
You have heard my story. Now, if you can tell what else
of future pain I have, reveal it. And do not
because of pity soothe me with false words. I say
insincere speeches are a most shameful malady.

CHORUS

Oh, cease, alas!
I had never thought, O never, that such strange words

would come to my hearing,
never that things so hard to be seen, so hard
to be borne would be hurting my heart with the double edge
of a goad,—desolation, distraction and terror.
O fate, fate, my blood runs cold
as I look on the fortunes of Io.

PROMETHEUS

Too soon you grieve and are like one that's full of fear.
Forbear till you have heard her future troubles too.

CHORUS

Speak, tell it all. For when one is sick it helps one
to know beforehand clearly what one must suffer.

PROMETHEUS

As for your first request, you have gained it from me
lightly, for first you wished to hear her own account
of the ordeal through which she has passed. Now listen
to the future, to the sufferings that this young girl
is fated still to undergo at Hera's hands.
And, child of Inachos, lay up these words of mine
within your heart, so you may learn your journey's end.
First, then, you must turn away from here to the rising
of the sun and go through lands that have not felt the plough.
You will reach the roving Scythians, who live raised up
above the ground in wattle huts that rest upon
the wheels of waggons. They are armed with long range bows.
Do not go near them. Turn your feet along the edge
of the salt-sounding shores and so go through their land.
Now on your left hand live the workers in iron,
the Chalybes, and of them too you must take care.
They are wild men, not fit for strangers to approach.
You will come to the river Hybristes, aptly named.

39

Do not cross over it, since it is hard to cross,
until you come to Caucasus itself, highest
of mountains, where the river pours away its might
from the very summit. And then you must pass over
star-neighbouring mountain tops, and set your foot upon
the road to the south, where you will reach the man-hating
host of the Amazons, who, in a time to come,
round Thermodon will inhabit Themiskyra
where Salmydessos lies, that rugged jaw of the sea,
no friend to sailors and to their ships a step-mother.
They will set you on your way and be glad to do it.
Then at the very narrows and gates of the sea
you will come to the Cimmerian strait. Leave this behind
bravely, and pass right out through the Maeotic channel.
And always among mortals there will be great talk
of your journey. The Bosporus will get its name
from you. So, when you have left the plain of Europe,
you will reach the land of Asia. Now, do you not think
that the dictator of the gods with all alike
deals violently? This mortal girl here he, a god,
craved for his love and laid these wanderings on her.
A bitter wooer you have found, my child, for this
marriage of yours. For the words which you have just heard
are to be thought of as hardly the beginning.

IO

Ah me! Alas! Ah me!

PROMETHEUS

Again you have cried out and sob away your breath.
What will you do when you have heard your future pain?

CHORUS

Can there be more pain for her that you will tell of?

PROMETHEUS

Indeed there can. A stormy sea of wicked woe.

IO

What then do I gain from living? Why did I not at once
throw myself headlong from this rugged rock, and so,
dashed to the earth, I might from all these pains of mine
have won my freedom. It is better to die once
than to suffer wretchedly throughout one's every day.

PROMETHEUS

It would be hard indeed for you to bear my pains,
since for me death is not permitted by the fates.
That would have been to find freedom from my trouble;
but now there lies before me no end to my labours
until the time Zeus falls from his dictatorship.

IO

Is it possible that Zeus will one day fall from power?

PROMETHEUS

You would be glad, I imagine, to see that happen.

IO

How should I not be, I who suffer ill from Zeus?

PROMETHEUS

What I say is true, and you may learn the truth of it.

IO

And who will take from Zeus the sceptre of his power?

PROMETHEUS

He will himself, he and his empty-headed plans.

41

IO

In what way? Tell me, if it does no harm to speak.

PROMETHEUS

He will make the sort of marriage that one day he'll rue.

IO

With a god or with a mortal? Say, if it may be told.

PROMETHEUS

What does it matter whom? I may not tell of this.

IO

Will it be by his wife that he will lose his throne?

PROMETHEUS

Yes. The son she'll bear will be better than his father.

IO

Has he no means by which to turn away this fate?

PROMETHEUS

No means at all, except if I were free from bondage.

IO

And who, against the will of Zeus, shall set you free?

PROMETHEUS

One of your children is destined to be my saviour.

IO

What's this? A child of mine will free you from your pain?

PROMETHEUS

Third in descent after ten generations more.

This prophecy is now no longer plain to judge.

PROMETHEUS

And do not seek to know your own pains to the end.

IO

You must not offer me kindness and then withhold it.

PROMETHEUS

I have two tales to tell and I will tell you one.

IO

What are they? Say, and give me power to choose which one.

PROMETHEUS

I will. Choose then whether I shall tell you clearly
of your future troubles or of him who will free me.

CHORUS

Be pleased to gratify her with one of your tales
and me with the other. Do not grudge us your story.
Tell her of the wandering she has still to do.
and me of him who will free you. I long to hear.

PROMETHEUS

If this is what you wish for, I will not refuse
to tell you everything of what you want to know.
First, Io, I will tell of your sad wandering.
Inscribe this in the mindful tablets of your heart.
When you have passed the stream that bounds two continents
go on towards the fire-faced and sun-trodden dawn,
crossing the roaring of the sea, until you come
to the Gorgon lowlands of Kisthene. Here there dwell

the children of Phorkis, three old unmarried hags,
swan shaped, and having a single eye between them,
and a single tooth. On them the sun never looks down
with rays from high, nor ever does the moon by night.
And near to them are dwelling their three winged sisters,
the Gorgons with their snaky hair, hated by men,
for no mortal can see them and not cease to breathe.
This is the sort of guard I say is set for you.
Now here's another sight that's hard for you to face.
You must beware of Zeus's sharp-beaked raging hounds,
the griffins, and the one-eyed host of cavalry
from Arimaspia who dwell beside a stream
rolling with gold that is in the path of Pluto.
Do not go near them. Afterwards you will arrive
in a far land, among black people, those who dwell
by the Aithiops and by the fountains of the sun.
Go on along that river's bank until you come
to a wanderfall, where from the Bibline mountains down
the Nile lets loose his holy and his pleasant stream.
This stream will guide you to the triangular country
of Nile-land. And here, Io, at last you are fated,
you and your children, to found your far-off settlement.
If any of this is indistinct and difficult for you,
go back to it again, and clearly learn it all.
I have more time to pass than I would like to have.

CHORUS

If you have any more to tell her or anything
left out in your account of her heart-breaking way,
then say it. But if you have told it all, then give
to us the gift we asked and you, no doubt, recall.

PROMETHEUS

She has heard the whole of her journey to the end.

44

But, to show her that she has not listened in vain,
I will tell her of what she went through before she came here,
and give this story as evidence for my account.
I shall leave aside the greater part of the tale
and come to what was the end of the path you trod.
It was after you had come to the Molossian plains,
then to Dodona of the craggy ridges, where
are both Thesprotian Zeus's prophetic seat
and, an incredible wonder, the talking oak trees.
Beneath these trees, clearly and in no riddling words,
you were declared one who, in the future, would be
the famous wife of Zeus. Does this part stir your heart?
Then driven by the fly, you darted on your way
beside the sea and towards the great gulf of Rhea,
from which you were driven back and forced to retrace
your steps. But in the future that bay of the sea,
you may be sure of it, will be called 'Ionian,'
a memorial among all men of your journey.
This I have said as a proof of my intelligence,
how it sees rather further than what is evident.
The rest I shall tell to you and to her alike,
now back upon the path of what I said before.
There is a city called Kanobos, at the end
of the world, at the very mouth and bar of the Nile.
And there at last Zeus gives you back your wits again,
with just a touch and stroke of hand that brings no fear.
Then, named from this manner of Zeus's impregnation,
Your son will be black Epaphos,[1] and he will have
the harvest of the land watered by Nile's broad stream.
From him in the fifth generation comes a family
of fifty women, who, against their will, will come
once more to Argos, fleeing a kindred wedding

[1] Derived from a verb meaning 'to touch lightly.'

with cousins, who, their hearts trembling with passion,
falcons, not left far behind in the chase by doves,
will come pursuing marriage that is not to be
pursued. God will grudge them the bodies of their wives.
Pelasgia will receive them with the kind of war
where women kill. They will be subdued by daring
that watches in the night. For every wife will take
her husband's life, and stain her two-edged sword in blood,
Such Love as this I pray may come upon my foes.
And yet desire will so melt one of these girls
as not to kill her bedfellow. Her purpose will be
made blunt, and, out of her two choices, she will wish
rather to be called irresolute than a murderess.
And she will give birth to a race of kings in Argos.
To tell of all this clearly would need many words;
however, from her family will come a child,
bold, famous for the bow, and he it is who will
free me from suffering. This, then, was the prophecy
my aged mother, Titan Themis, told to me.
How it will be fulfilled and by what means requires
long time to tell, nor would you gain by learning it.

10

Away! Away!
Again it begins, sudden pain and a crazy
madness to urge me. The sting of the fly
burns without fire.
My heart in distraction beats at my breast.
With rolling eyes, my vision whirling,
out of my path by the raging breath
of madness driven, I lose control
of speech, and murky words go beating idly
on the waves of a doom I hate.

[*Exit Io.*]

Wise, very wise was he
who first found this ring true within his judgment
and with his tongue gave out the word:
far the best thing is to wed within one's station,
and, if one works for one's living, not to long
for marriage with the glorious in wealth
or with the families whose pride is birth.

Never, O never, O
powerful Fates, may you behold me coming
to share the bed of Zeus. Let me
never be brought in marriage near to one of the
heavenly gods. I shrink as I see the loveless
maidenhood of Io, beaten down
by cruel wandering curse of pain from Hera.

For me, when marriage is well matched there is
nothing to fear. But let no eye of the gods
greater than I, ineluctable, perceive me.
That is a war when fighting does no good,
an arsenal of helplessness. I cannot tell
what would become of me. I do not see
how I could flee from what Zeus has devised.

PROMETHEUS

I swear to you that Zeus, for all his stubborn mind,
will yet be lowly; such a marriage is it that he plans
to make, one that will hurl him from his dictatorship,
a thing of nothing from his throne. The curse of Kronos
his father then indeed will come true utterly,
that curse he made when hurled from his established throne.
And from these troubles no one of the gods but I
can clearly show him how he can escape. I know

the means and how to accomplish it. And therefore now
let him sit confident, and in his airy noise
put faith, and brandish in his hands the fire-breathed bolt.
In no way will all this avail him to escape
falling into shame an intolerable fall.
So mighty is the wrestler that now he seeks
to equip against himself, an invincible wonder,
one that will find a mightier flame than the lightning,
and heavy crashes that go beyond the thunder.
And as for that plague of the sea that shakes the earth,
Poseidon's spear, the trident, he will brush it aside.
Zeus, stumbling on this misadventure, will find out
how far apart are supreme power and slavery.

CHORUS

What you would have yourself you mouth out against Zeus.

PROMETHEUS

I say what will come true and also what I wish.

CHORUS

Then must we look for one to hold power over Zeus?

PROMETHEUS

Yes, and pains for Zeus more hard to escape than these.

CHORUS

Do you not cower in fear when you let loose such words?

PROMETHEUS

What should I fear, I who am not fated to die?

CHORUS

Yet he might bring on you a trial still worse than this.

48

Then let him. I can imagine all that's possible.

CHORUS

Those who bow down to Adrasteia show wisdom.

PROMETHEUS

Do honour, pray and fawn upon the powers that be.
As for me, Zeus matters to me less than nothing.
He is free to act and free to reign for this short time
just as he wills, since not for long he'll rule the gods.
But here I see coming the messenger of Zeus,
the agent of the newly-established dictator.
I am sure that he has come with something new to tell.

[*Enter Hermes*]

HERMES

You there, the clever one, and too sharp in your sharpness,
the one who sinned against the gods by giving over
honour to creatures of a day, you thief of fire,
the father orders you to tell of that marriage
in which you boast and by which he will fall from power.
And also none of this must be said in riddles;
tell all of it straight out, and do not put on me,
Prometheus, a double journey back. You are aware
Zeus is not softened by such people as you are.

PROMETHEUS

Proud-mouthed indeed they are and full of arrogance
such words as these for a lackey of gods to speak.
You and your power are young, and so, no doubt, you think
you dwell in towers where grief can never come. And yet
have I not seen dictators twice hurled down from them?

Yes, and this third one, ruling now, I shall see fall
most sudden in dishonour. Do I look as though
I cowered and shrunk away in fear from these young gods?
I am far, yes, very far indeed from that. Now you
go back again over the road you came upon,
since you will hear from me none of the things you ask..

HERMES

Before now it was by a self-conceit like this
you brought and settled yourself among these sufferings.

PROMETHEUS

For your menial position I would not exchange
my own ill fortune. You may be sure of that.

HERMES

No doubt it is better to be a menial to this rock
than to be the trusted messenger of father Zeus.

PROMETHEUS

Insolent words are right where you find insolence.

HERMES

It seems that you take pride in what is happening to you.

PROMETHEUS

Take pride? I wish that I could see my enemies
take pride like this, and among them I reckon you.

HERMES

Me? Do you blame me at all for your disaster?

Simply I am an enemy to all the gods.
I helped them, and they persecute me causelessly.

HERMES

You speak like a madman, brain-sick seriously.

PROMETHEUS

Yes, sick, if it is sickness to detest one's foes.

HERMES

You would not be tolerable if you were fortunate.

PROMETHEUS

Alas!

HERMES

That is a word Zeus does not understand.

PROMETHEUS

Yet Time, as Time grows old, instructs in everything.

HERMES

Though you do not yet know how to behave wisely.

PROMETHEUS

If I did, I would not have spoken to you, you lackey.

HERMES

It seems you will say nothing of what the father wants.

PROMETHEUS

I am his debtor and would like to pay him back.

HERMES

So then you laugh at me as if I was a child.

PROMETHEUS

Yes, are you not a child and still more foolish than a child,
if you expect to hear of anything from me?
There is no shame and no kind of device by which
Zeus can induce me ever to reveal these things,
until he loosens these despiteful chains of mine.
And so let all his burning flame be hurled at me,
and with the white-winged snow and subterranean
thunders let him confound and mingle everything.
None of all this will bend me so that I will tell
by whom he is bound to be thrown from his dictatorship.

HERMES

Now, look. Does this seem likely to be helpful to you?

PROMETHEUS

It has been looked to and decided long ago.

HERMES

You fool, have the courage, in the end have courage
to frame your thought correctly to your present ills.

PROMETHEUS

Your sooothing words beat on me vainly like a wave.
Let it not come into your head that I shall fear
ever the will of Zeus and have a woman's mind,
and be a suppliant to him I greatly hate,
with womanish up-turnings of the hands, that he
might loose me from these chains. I am wholly different.

HERMES

It seems that, speaking, I should speak a lot in vain.
You are neither soft at all nor melted by my prayers,

but, taking the bit between your teeth, like a colt
not broken in, you try and fight against the rein.
Yet all this overkeenness comes from a weak design.
Stubbornness, in a mind whose thoughts have gone astray,
has in its simple self less strength than anything.
And now, if you are not persuaded by my words,
consider what a storm and hurricane of ill
will fall upon you past escape. For, first of all,
with thunder and with lightning flash the father will
tear up this rocky gully, will hide your body
beneath, and arms of stone will fold you round about.
And so you will pass through a lengthy stretch of time,
and then come back again into the light. And now
Zeus's winged hound, the blood-red eagle, greedily
will tear into great rags the flesh of your body,
coming, although not asked, to dinner every day,
and he will feast upon and gnaw your liver black.
And do not look for any end to pains like these,
until a god appears to take upon himself
your load of suffering, and is willing to go down
to rayless Hades and the gloomy depths of Hell.
And now make up your mind. Be sure these words of mine
are no pretended boasting, but too clearly true.
The mouth of Zeus does not know how to tell a lie:
no, he will bring his every word to act. Now you
look closely to yourself, reflect, and do not think
self-will can ever be a better thing than good advice.

CHORUS

To us it seems that Hermes' speech is to the point.
What he commends to you is to relax from your
self-will and seek the wisdom that's in good advice.
Do as he says, since wrong is shameful in the wise.

53

PROMETHEUS

I tell you I know this news that he cries to me,
nor is there any shame in the suffering
an enemy feels at the hands of his enemies.
Therefore on me now let the double-edged
curling of fire be loosed! Let air
rage in anger with thunder and roaring
of savage winds! Let a blast blow
to make earth's depths totter down to their roots!
In ungentle surge let it heap together
waves of the sea in a mass and the paths of the
heavenly stars! Let it raise my body
high, and in whirlwind of strong compulsion,
hurl it down into Hell! Zeus cannot
any way put me to death.

HERMES

What is this but to listen to madmen's
words and devices?
This man's prayer is no different from raving.
He cannot relax from his frenzy.
You, then, at least, who sympathise with him
in his suffering, take yourselves elsewhere,
away from this place.
See that your wits are not driven crazy by
terrible roaring of thunder.

CHORUS

Say something else, or give me advice
that is able to move me. You cannot suppose
I can endure this wild word you've spoken.
How can you urge me to follow the coward's way?
With him I am willing to suffer what must be,
since I have learnt to hate all traitors;

there exists no disease
that I loathe more than that one.

HERMES

Well, then, remember what I tell you
and do not, when you are chased by destruction,
find fault with fortune. Do not ever
say that Zeus has thrown you to suffering
unforeseen. It is not so. You brought it
all on yourselves. For with clear knowledge,
neither suddenly nor by deception,
you will be folded up by your folly
in an infinite net of destruction.

[*Thunder, lightning and earthquake. Prometheus and the rock to which he is bound gradually sink out of sight.*]

PROMETHEUS

Now it is fact, and no longer in words
that the earth is convulsed.
Out of the deep the roaring of thunder
rolls past, and flickering fire of the lightning
flashes out, and the whirlwinds
roll up the dust, and the blasts of all storms
leap at each other, declaring
a war of the winds,
and the air and the sea are confounded.
These, most clearly, are strokes from Zeus
coming upon me to cause me fear.
O my glorious mother, O Heaven
with circle of light that is common to everyone,
you see me and see this injustice.